SCHOOL'S OUT!

Compiled by John Foster
with illustrations by
Alastair Graham

CLASS: 821.008

No. J05291

AUTHOR	SUBJECT	DATE
		1988

D1643070

Oxford U

EVERETT

J05291F1848

OXFORD
UNIVERSITY PRESS

Great Clarendon Street, Oxford OX2 6DP

Oxford University Press is a department of the University of
Oxford. It furthers the University's objective of excellence in
research, scholarship, and education by publishing worldwide in

Oxford New York
Athens Auckland Bangkok Bogotá Buenos Aires Cape Town
Chennai Dar es Salaam Delhi Florence Hong Kong Istanbul Karachi
Kolkata Kuala Lumpur Madrid Melbourne Mexico City Mumbai Nairobi
Paris São Paulo Shanghai Singapore Taipei Tokyo Toronto Warsaw

with associated companies in Berlin Ibadan

OXFORD is a trade mark of Oxford University Press

© John L. Foster 1988

First published 1988
Reprinted in hardback 1988, 1990
Reprinted in paperback 1988, 1989, 1990, 1991, 1992, 1994, 1995, 1996
Reprinted in paperback with new cover 1998 (twice), 1999, 2001

All rights reserved. No part of this publication may be reproduced,
stored in a retrieval system, or transmitted, in any form or by any means,
electronic, mechanical, photocopying, recording, or otherwise, without
the prior permission of Oxford University Press.

This book is sold subject to the condition that it shall not, by way
of trade or otherwise, be lent, re-sold, hired out or otherwise circulated
without the publisher's prior consent in any form of binding or cover
other than that in which it is published and without a similar condition
including this condition being imposed on the subsequent purchaser.

British Library Cataloguing in Publication Data available

1. Children's poetry, English. 2. Schools—
Juvenile poetry
I. Foster. John L. (John Louis)
821'.008'0355 PR1195.C47

ISBN 0-19-276078-5 paperback

Cover illustration by Nick Sharratt

Printed in Great Britain by
Cox & Wyman Ltd, Reading, Berkshire

Contents

MARBLES AMONG THE TREE ROOTS

SCRAPED CHALK SHRIEKS AND WHISPERS CREEP

YOU'RE STANDING ON A STRAWBERRY

NEVER SAY BOO! TO A MOUSE

BEWARE OF THE HISTORY TEACHER

AN ILL WIND THAT NO ONE BLOWS GOOD

WHERE DO ALL THE TEACHERS GO?

SCHOOLDAYS COME IN SQUARES

Schoolspeak

's cool, man,
It's the best.
Gotta keep your interest
Talkin' is the name of the game
And if you wanna play
You gotta speak the same:
SCHOOLSPEAK,
's cool, man,
Understand me if you can.
P.E.'s brill,
Maths is vile,
Maths, man, it ain't my style.
Art's a doddle,
R.E.'s a doss,
Gotta show 'em who's the boss:
SCHOOLSPEAK,
's cool, man,
It's the lingo they wanna ban.
Science is grotty,
Drama's dead good,
History I'd skive, if I could.
English is ace,
French is a bind,
I'd love to leave this class behind:
SCHOOLSPEAK,
's cool, man,
's all part of my master plan.
Miss is magic,
Sir's a pain,
Head's a wally, librarian's plain,
Dinners are skill,
Homework's a drag
I'm telling you school ain't my bag.
SCHOOLSPEAK
SCHOOL, MAN,
's cool.

Ray Mather

Look out!

The witches mumble horrid chants,
You're scolded by five thousand aunts,
   A Martian pulls a fearsome face
   And hurls you into Outer Space,
You're tied in front of whistling trains,
A tomahawk has sliced your brains,
   The tigers snarl, the giants roar,
   You're sat on by a dinosaur.
In vain you're shouting 'Help' and 'Stop',
The walls are spinning like a top,
   The earth is melting in the sun
   And all the horror's just begun.
And, oh, the screams, the thumping hearts –
That awful night before school starts.

Max Fatchen

I don't want to go to school

I don't want to go to school Mum
I want to stay at home with my duck.
I'd rather stay at home with you Mum,
And hit the skirting board with my truck.
Don't make me go to school today Mum,
I'll sit here quiet on the stairs
Or I'll sit underneath the table
Scratching all the varnish off the chairs.

I don't want to go to school Mum
When I could be underneath your feet.
It's shopping day and we could go together
Taking twice as long to get to Regent Street.
And every time you stop to talk to someone
I won't let you concentrate, no fear,
I'll be jumping up and down beside you
Shouting, 'Can I have some sweets Mum?' in your ear.

Or how about me doing a bit of painting?
Or what about a bit of cutting out?
Or sitting in the open bedroom window,
Body in and legs sticking out?
Or what about us going up the park Mum?
Or how about me sitting at the sink?
Or what about me making you a cake Mum?
And Mum. Hey Mum. Mum can I have a drink?

And Mum, Mum what's that at the bottom of the cupboard?
And Mum, what's in the bag you put down there?
And hey Mum watch me jump straight off the sofa,
And Mum, whose dog is that stood over there?
What you doing Mum? Peeling potatoes?
Sit me on the drainer watching you
I wouldn't *mind* me trousers getting wet Mum.
Oh I aren't half fed up. What can I do?

What time is Daddy coming home Mum?
What's in that long packet? Sausagemeat?
How long is it before he comes Mum?
And Mum. Hey Mum. What can I have to eat?
Oh sorry Mum! I've upset me Ribena.
Oh look! It's making quite a little pool.
Hey Mum, hey, where we going in such a hurry?
Oh Mum! Hey Mum, you're taking me to SCHOOL!

Pam Ayres

August poem

Today it is raining
and it is autumn.

The children are going back to school with their new bags
and their new uniforms.

It is spring for the children and autumn for the teachers.

For the children are always young and the teachers are
        growing older
and the blackboard is grainy with chalk.

The teachers look out at the rainy playground
and sometimes they think about *Macbeth*
but mostly about their own lives
and how the freshness of spring has departed.

It is raining
and it is autumn,
and the rain prickles the sea
and wets the new uniforms of the children
and their new shoes.

When it is raining the soul becomes grey,
a continuous drizzle of autumn.
It is like a screen that will always be there.

The teachers look out, the forgotten chalk in their hands,
and they break it over and over.

Iain Crichton Smith

New boy

The day began with tea.
I was wearing flannel shorts
Which rubbed my knees leaving
A ring of red beneath the grey.
We sat, my parents and I,
At a polished table
Drinking pale tea
Amongst unfamiliar faces.
There was cake
And side plates and knives
And my toes felt cramped
Inside tight black shoes.

My parents were quiet,
Father in a suit,
Mother with her best brooch
And new handbag.
We children were excused
So we gathered acorns
Beneath a tree
Near some frayed ropes.

We did not hear the cars leave.

We found ourselves in
Narrow beds,
Watching the shadows,
Trying hard not to cry
And waiting for sleep.

Nigel Cox

47 Bus

We're doing nothing new in Maths
If I stay at home with a cold today
And if I miss a History test
I know it all backwards anyway;

We've had the lessons I like for the week:
There's nothing with which I couldn't cope
And if it isn't in the book
Someone will lend me the notes;

But when I remember how early
Some other people have to get up,
Like the invisible man, the milkman,
Ghosting round in his electric truck,

And the way that Four Lane Ends
At 8.15 is a regular date
Where, rain or hail or snow or shine,
The three of us always wait,

Though I've hardly time for breakfast
And while I must seem ridiculous
To pass up the chance of a well-earned rest,
I mustn't disappoint the 47 bus.

Stanley Cook

Bus

Jane caught the school bus,
    and so did Melissa.
Bill was a professional
    hitch-hiking bus-misser.

Ian Serraillier

Early bird does catch the fattest worm

Late again
going to be late again
for school again
and I can't say
I overslept
can't blame it
on the bus
can't blame it
on the train
can't blame it
on the rain
and Granny words
buzzing in my brain
'Early bird does catch the worm,'
and I thinking
Teacher going tell me off
and I wishing
I was a bird
and teacher was a juicy worm.

John Agard

Monday

Monday; not only that but it's pouring;
My friend's away and that'll be boring;
Games are off, in Maths there's a test –
It's a day when I never do my best.
No one thinks it's a bumper-fun day –
So why don't we simply cancel Monday?

It's a day when teachers speak a faceful:
'This work is really quite disgraceful!'
And Monday lunch just breaks your heart:
It's green grub salad and concrete tart.
It's Monday again, a proper blues day:
Couldn't we just begin on Tuesday?

Eric Finney

Some days

Some days this school
is a huge concrete sandwich
squeezing me out like jam.

It weighs so much
breathing hurts, my legs freeze
my body is heavy.

On days like that
I carry whole buildings
high on my back.

Other days
the school is a rocket
thrusting right into the sun.

It's yellow and green
freshly painted,
the cabin windows
gleam with laughter.

On days like that
whole buildings support me,
my ladder is pushing
over their rooftops.

Amongst the clouds
I'd need a computer
to count all the bubbles
bursting aloud in my head.

David Harmer

SCOO-WOOL— THE HIPPIEST TIME OF YOUR LIFE

Lining up

Lining up to go in school is
Boring.
But you can say one thing . . .
While you wait
You can have a little sleep
Standing up
Like a horse,
And, of course,
You can watch the field
Of young barley.

I've told no one about the field,
But when the wind
Slips down the hill
It blows soft grey hollows of barley green
In the fur of the field,
Like the fur on a cat's back,
On Lucy's back when I round my lips and blow
Shallow saucers of fluid softness
Along her spine.

It is five to nine,
I'm the end of the queue;
I hear Mr Baxter yell,
'Hi, you!'
He threatens me with the bell
And I jump out of my quiet shell
And run to catch up with the end of the line.

Gregory Harrison

Late

You're late, said miss.
The bell has gone,
dinner numbers done
and work begun.

What have you got to say for yourself?

Well, it's like this, miss.
Me mum was sick,
me dad fell down the stairs,
the wheel fell off me bike
and then we lost our Billy's snake
behind the kitchen chairs. Earache
struck down me grampy, me gran
took quite a funny turn.
Then on the way I met this man
whose dog attacked me shin –
look miss, you can see the blood,
it doesn't look too good,
does it?

Yes, yes, sit down –
and next time say you're sorry
for disturbing all the class.
Now get on with your story,
fast!

Please miss, I've got nothing to write about.

Judith Nicholls

It's the thought that counts

'I brought these in for assembly,'
and he handed over his offering
of crisp red tulips with raggedy stems.
But Tom never had flowers to bring.

'Thank you, Tom,' his teacher said,
'But where . . . ?' she asked with care;
'Maybe they came from my garden,'
he smiled. 'Honest, Miss Adair!'

Tom sensed it wasn't going down
too well, so he had another go.
'Maybe my mum bought them for me.'
'No, Tom. I don't think so.'

It had all seemed so easy this
morning when on his way to school,
but now there were all these questions
and he knew Miss Adair was no fool.

'Come on, Tom,' she coaxed him,
'Tell me and we'll say no more.'
'Maybe I picked them in the park,
maybe . . .' He looked at the floor.

'Thank you, Tom. Don't do it again.'
She half hid the smile on her face.
When the children went into assembly
Tom's tulips had pride of place!

Moira Andrew

Morning assembly

I want to know why when we gather for prayers,
When nobody chatters and nobody dares
To scratch at their knee, say hello, turn their head
While the passage from Scripture is being read . . .

Why, when everyone else's head is bowed
And all the rest scarcely can breathe aloud,
Why, during the prayer when our eyes are tight shut,
Mister X and Miss Y share a chocolate and nut?

How do I know? I admit I was sly
For I took just a peep with just half of one eye –
Mister X and Miss Y whispered, nodded and smiled
In a way that's forbidden if you are a child.

It puzzles and frets me . . . the rules don't apply
To teachers and parents I think with a sigh.
I must squeeze up my eyes or the Lord will condemn,
So why ain't he angry and furious with them?

Gregory Harrison

First art lesson

My new paintbox's shining black lacquer lid
divided neatly into three oblong sections
reflects my funny face, the art room windows
white with autumn clouds and flecked with rain.

When I open it, the scented white enamel dazzles.
Inside, pure colours are displayed like blocks
of a bulb-grower's beds of flowers, toy spectrum
in china tubs and tin tubes, a cubist rainbow.

From my jam jar filled with fresh water at the sink
I pour a little liquid into each depression;
take the brush of silky camel hair; wet its plumpness
for the first time, and the last, between my lips.

Then dip its fine, dark tip into the water-tanks,
and into juicy wells of Crimson Lake, Gamboge, Sienna,
Peacock Blue, Burnt Ochre, Emerald, Olive, Terracotta,
Vermilion, Umber, Cadmium, Indigo, Intense Black.

Damp the paper. From the top edge, with sleek, loaded brush,
begin to release the first phantom of a pale-blue wash.

James Kirkup

Scoo-wool – the hippiest time of your life

In the art class I happened to mention
I'd rather be drawing a pension.
The result of my wit
Was they all threw a fit
And now I've got a detention!

At Inglish I reely eck-sell
From my rightin I'm shore you ken tell
An' even my teecher
Sez 'No wun can beecher
For their's hardly a werd yoo carnt spell.'

The French class dissolve into grins
When I'm guilty of translation sins
But I certainly know a
'Coup de Grace' is a mower
And 'Pas de Deux's' father of twins.

Chemistry's all part of learning
And interesting for the discerning.
But our teacher named Corbett
Blew himself into orbit
Leaving only the faint smell of burning.

Physics is a bit of a bore
And I don't think I'll learn any more
In a storm our instructor
Touched a lightning conductor
And is now brown and crisp on the floor.

Our woodwork instructor'll bore yer
For most times he tends to ignore yer
Until 'You, over there!
You cut the legs off my chair
No need to deny it, I sawyer!'

Philip C. Gross

Drama lesson

'Let's see some super shapes you blue group,'
Mr Lavender shouts down the hall;
'And forests don't forget your trembly leaves
And stand up straight and tall.'

But I've got Phillip Chubb in our group
And he wants to be Robin Hood,
And Ann Boots' sulking 'cos she's not with her friend
And I don't see why I should be wood.

The lights are switched on in the classrooms
Outside the sky's nearly black
And the dining hall smells of gravy and cabbage
And Phillip Chubb has boils down his back.

Sir tells Chubb that's he's got to be tree,
But he won't wave his arms around;
He says, 'How can I wave me branches sir,
When someone has chopped them all down?'

Then I come galloping through Sherwood
Following my destiny
And I really believe I'm Robin Hood
Come to set Maid Marion free.

At my back I feel my long bow,
My broad sword clanks at my side,
My outlaws gallop close behind
As into adventure we ride.

'Untie that maid you villain,' I shout,
With all the strength I have,
But the tree has got bored and is picking his nose
And Maid Marion has gone to the lav.

After rehearsals, Sir calls us together
And each group performs its play
But just as it comes to our turn
The bell goes for the end of the day.

As I trudge my way home through the suburbs
The cars and the houses retreat
And the thunder of hooves beats in my mind
As I gallop through acres of wheat.

The castle gleams white in the distance
Her banner flaps golden and red
And unheard trumpets weave silver dreams
In the landscapes of my head.

Gareth Owen

Partners

Find a partner,
says sir, and sit
with him or her.
A whisper here,
a shuffle there,
a rush of feet.
One pair,
another pair,
till twenty-four
sit safely on the floor
and all are gone
but one –
who stands,
like stone,
and waits;
tall,
still,
alone.

Judith Nicholls

Blame

Graham, look at Maureen's leg,
She says you tried to tattoo it!
I did, Miss, yes – with my biro,
But Jonathan told me to do it.

Graham, look at Peter's sock,
It's got a burn-hole through it!
It was just an experiment, Miss, with the lens.
Jonathan told me to do it.

Alice's bag is stuck to the floor,
Look, Graham, did you glue it?
Yes, but I never thought it would work,
And Jonathan told me to do it.

Jonathan, what's all this I hear
About you and Graham Prewitt?
Well, Miss, it's really more his fault:
He *tells* me to tell him to do it!

                                        Allan Ahlberg

It's not my fault

It's not my fault
It isn't fair
It's not my gum
In Jenny's hair

It wasn't me
I didn't do it
The brick was his
I know he threw it

I wasn't there
What broken dish?
It's not my turn
To feed the fish

What missing sweets?
Which chocolate cake?
I didn't push her
In the lake

It isn't fair
Why pick on me?
When I leave school
Just wait and see

John Kitching

Ben

Ben's done something really bad,
He's forged a letter from his dad.
He's scrawled:

Dear Miss,
    Please let Ben be
Excused this week from all P.E.
He's got a bad cold in his chest,
And so I think it might be best,
If he throughout this week could be
Excused from doing all P.E.
I hope my writing's not too bad,
    yours sincerely,
        (signed)
            Ben's Dad.

Colin West

Fear

I was afraid of the wall bars.
Sometimes, we managed
physical jerks without them.
Then, a call
sharp and peremptory
would come, commanding
'Run to the wall bars!
Climb! Swing out – and fall!'

I ran with the others –
climbed, and hung suspended
my face to the wall
just urging myself to drop.
But I couldn't.
Imagination held me captive
at its usual centre,
and there I had to stop.

Below me, there wasn't a six foot gap
and safety
with rubbery gym shoes
plump on the polished floor,
but a primal cliff
of terrifying dimensions
and beneath it
the slavering ocean's hungry roar.

So the others fell
and leaped to a tidy posture
hands to their sides
and eyes excited with fun,
while I wrenched my fingers
away from the wooden structure
sensing, like Gloucester,
a cliff
where there wasn't one.

Jean Kenward

Changing gear

'Don't forget your swimming things –
    Hurry, here's the bus!
We can't keep it waiting.
    Rush, boy, rush!'

Out of the school, into the bus,
    First to the pool he dashes,
Inside the changing room
    Dizzily undresses,

Opens up his plastic bag,
    Tumbles out the loot –
Shorts, shirt, pads
    And a football boot.

Ian Serraillier

Swimming lesson

I hate Wednesdays . . .
We go on the bus to the baths instead of gym
And I can't swim.

I hate the smell of the water
Lapping the white-tiled rim;
I hate the painful, burning sting
Of water up my nose,
And the throbbing pressure ring
Inside my ears.
Of course, you can't see tears
Under water . . .
I can't see anything.
How can the other kids
Flutter open protecting lids
And actually see?
It doesn't happen to me.
And how can the other kids enclose
Elbows and knees and heels and toes
Inside a dolphin shape and dive
With a trail of bubbles
And come up alive?
It can't possibly happen to me.

I hate the noise of banging doors,
And skidding on the slippery floors,
The end-of-lesson scrambling rush,
The bus-is-waiting breathless push,
The struggling with twisted socks
On wet feet in a tiny box,
The teacher snarling, 'You are late;
Do hurry, child, the bus can't wait.'
I hate each smug Olympic hope
Gliding through water where I grope
What use being fairly good at Maths
If hopeless in the swimming-baths?

I just hate Wednesdays . . .
All right for him and him and him,
But I can't swim.

Gregory Harrison

Kieran

Kieran can't walk like the rest of us.
He comes to school on the special bus.
He has to use crutches to get about
And he's fast, but he can't keep up when we run
When we race in the wind and fight and have fun
He can't keep up, he has to shout
'Wait for me, everyone, wait for me.'
And sometimes we wait, and sometimes we
Run off and hide, and that's when he
Sits in the yard with his sticks on the ground
Sits by himself until he's found
By Sir, or Miss, and they sit and talk
And we watch them laugh in a special way
And we'd love to know what he has to say
About the ones who ran away.
The ones who forgot that he can't walk.
And then we remember to ask him to play
And we kick the ball and he hits it back;
He's quick with those sticks, he has the knack
Of whamming the ball right into goal.
And if he falls over he doesn't fuss,
We hoist him back up and we laugh at the soil
On his hands and his face, and give him his sticks.
He's strong when he fights us, but he never kicks –
He can't use his legs like the rest of us.
He comes to school on the special bus.

Berlie Doherty

32

King of the toilets

Maurice was King of the Toilets,
The ones by the wall – by the shed,
He ruled with the power and conviction
Of a king with a crown on his head.

He entered them first every morning
And he'd sit on the wall by the gate
And wait for the grumpy schoolkeeper
To unlock them – at twenty past eight.

Then he'd rush in with great shouts of triumph
And he'd slam all the doors one by one
And he'd climb on the caretaker's cupboards
And he'd pull all the chains just for fun.

He'd swing on the pipes by the cistern,
And he'd leap from the top of the doors,
And he'd frighten the new little infants –
With bellows and yellings and roars.

He always ate lunch in the toilets,
And he'd sit with his food on the floor,
And check who was coming (or going) –
And kick at the catch on their door.

He once burst the pipe by the outflow
By climbing right up on the tank,
And flooded the lower school library,
With water that gushed out and stank.

He once jammed the door on the end one
With five juniors stuck fast inside,
And bombed them with piles of old comics
Whilst they struggled and shouted and cried.

He was useless in class –
And at lessons.
He couldn't do hardly a thing –
But when he was out in the toilets –
THEN MAURICE THE USELESS WAS KING!

Peter Dixon

The hole in the hall

It started just like any other day.
We had assembly. We sang.
We walked back to our rooms.

The day the hole
appeared in the hall.

At ten o'clock
we heard a noise.
We could no longer see the piano,

the day the hole
appeared in the hall.

The head sent a girl to look.
She never came back.
I got her pencils,

the day the hole
appeared in the hall.

The head sent a teacher to look.
He never came back.
I got his pencils,

the day the hole
appeared in the hall.

So the head sent me to look.
I never came back.

I'm writing you this
from the hole in the hall
with one of my pencils.

I'm learning the piano.

Sometimes my parents
stand at the edge
telling me to come home
out of the hole
the hole in the hall,

but I'm happy in the hole.
I've got to know the teacher
(he's called Alan)
and the girl
(she's called Julie).

I play the piano
and we sing.

This is our favourite song:
'Here we are in the hole
the hole in the hall,
having a ball
in the hole in the hall
and we'll never come out
of the hole in the hall
at all.'

Ian McMillan and Martyn Wiley

Zonky Zizzibug

I've just appeared in this classroom.
I did not use the door.
I *have* just materialized
Through the classroom floor.

Do *not* call me a liar.
Do *not* call me a cheat.
No, teacher cannot see me,
Sitting in this seat.

My name *is* Zonky Zizzibug.
I don't know why you laugh.
This book is not a comic,
It's an extra-terrestrial graph.

I don't care what you say.
Oh please don't be a bore!
I *did* just materialize.
I did *not* use the door.

I have an anti-matter,
Anti-gravity device.
I also have a pill
For turning schoolboys into mice.

Do not call me a liar.
Do not call me a cheat.
You are not imagining things.
Do not blame the heat.

I *have* been to Venus.
I *have* been to Mars.
I've even been to Uranus
And several other stars.

Of course my blood is green!
The aeriel on my head?
Oh that's just something
That stops me being dead.

How dare you laugh and scoff!
Shush. Everyone will hear.
Look, now teacher's giving you
A *very* funny stare.

I *won't* say I'm Zonky Zizzibug.
I *am* going to go away.
I'm only allowed to play on earth
For a single day.

I'm going to drift round the classroom.
I'm going to float up in the air.
Then I'm going back off home
Because laughing is not fair.

I won't become visible.
I won't float down from the shelf.
I do not care if teacher
Thinks you are talking to yourself.

Brian Patten

MARBLES AMONG THE TREE ROOTS

Can you keep a secret?

Mary, can you keep a secret? Promise not to tell.
Cross your heart or die! Don't tell Wendy.

Wendy, can you keep a secret? Promise not to tell.
Cross your heart or die! Don't tell Jason.

Jason, can you keep a secret? Promise not to tell.
Cross your heart or die! Don't tell Darren.

Darren, can you keep a secret? Promise not to tell.
Cross your heart or die! Don't tell . . .

WHAT'S SO SPECIAL ABOUT YOUR CRUMMY, OLD
     SECRET THEN?

Ooh! You've spoilt it! I'm not going to tell you now!

David Jackson

Morning break

Andrew Flag plays football
Jane swings from the bars
Chucker Peach climbs drainpipes
Spike is seeing stars

Little Paul's a Martian
Anne walks on her toes
Ian Dump fights Kenny
Russell picks his nose

Dopey Di does hopscotch
Curly drives a train
Maddox-Brown and Thompson
Stuff shoes down the drain.

Lisa Thin throws netballs
Ranji stands and stares
Nuttall from the first year
Shouts and spits and swears

Dick Fish fires his ray gun
Gaz has stamps to swop
Dave and Dan are robbers
Teacher is the cop

Betty Blob pulls faces
Basher falls . . . and dies
Tracey shows her knickers
Loony swallows flies

Faye sits in a puddle
Trev is eating mud
Skinhead has a nose bleed
– pints and pints of blood

Robbo Lump pings marbles
Ahmed hands out cake
What a lot of nonsense
During
    Morning
        Break

Wes Magee

The outsider

The bell rings.
It is break. A shout
fiercely exultant
lets us out:
a tide of girls
a rush of boys
drawn
by a living tug of noise
from quiet study
and serene
to this explosive
space between
lesson and learning.
Wild, we are,
and vicious, too,
as cats at war:
kicking and plunging,
shouting, laying
strength, against strength –
the craft of playing.
Only the shy one
by the wall
stands, and will not
join in at all
but runs as straight
as summer rain
when the bell calls us
in again.

Jean Kenward

Playground game

As I went down the school yard
Down among the bullies, O,
They shouted at me good and hard
Kiss a girl and let her go.

And there were Mary, Ruth and Jean
Down among the bullies, O,
The prettiest girls you've ever seen
Kiss a girl and let her go.

Jean, Ruth and Mary gave a look so quick
Down among the bullies, O,
To see which one of them I'd pick
Kiss a girl and let her go.

The crowd stood round me like a wall
Down among the bullies, O,
I ran and dodged them one and all
Kiss a girl and let her go.

They cornered me by the cycle shed
Down among the bullies, O,
'Pick one of them or we'll punch your head!'
Kiss a girl and let her go.

I chose Kathy Brown with the mousy hair
Down among the bullies, O,
Who hadn't a boy and didn't care
Kiss a girl and let her go.

She thought she was ugly, Kathy Brown,
Down among the bullies, O,
Everyone thought I was playing the clown
Kiss a girl and let her go.

Our dry lips met for less than a second
  Down among the bullies, O,
The damage done will never be reckoned
  Kiss a girl and let her go.

Her eyes came alight as they'd never been
  Down among the bullies, O,
Their shadow fell on Mary, Ruth and Jean
  And the girl I kissed I'll never let go.

Raymond Wilson

Until the bell

Beyond the playground fence
Dogs are unleashed
And free they run.
Horses unbridled and free
Are barebacked in the sun.
The river slips the noose of weed
And free it flows to the sea.
Wind freed Coltsfoot seed,
Unchrysalid butterfly
Float free as birds,
As birds are flying
In cloud free sky
While I,
Fingers locked
In the mesh of the fence,
An inch away from the wild grass,
Must watch it all pass
Freewheeling by.

Julie Holder

Playtime in the fog

Fog drifted to school today
in a big grey ship.
Empty canvas flapped and sighed
ropes dripped with dew.

I pushed through the sailors,
all of them had goblin faces.
Ghostly hands ran silver fingers
down my spine, I shivered.

Ran towards my best friend
who turned into a Frankenstein
lumbering across the yard
his hands outstretched.

Strangled air let out a gasp,
one pale cloud of breath
whispered in my face.

Swooping back as Dracula
he gurgled round my damp cold neck
then flapped away.

The fog is thick and clammy.
I wish I could carve chunks of it,
I'd take them home to build
small grey igloos.

Two teachers pass,
they talk and dream of bells
booming out loud warnings
to ships stuck in a shifting sea.

David Harmer

Wet playtime

Wayne has lost his slippers
he left 'em on his chair
Liza Wilson saw 'em
at playtime they was there
Martin Doughty touched 'em
he threw them near the sink
he threw them in the corner
'cos he said they made a stink
Debbie saw him do it
and the dinner lady knows
she stood him in the corner
right next to Billy Rose.

The dinner lady's angry
the playground lady's cross
one's shouting in the lobby
and the other's caught Paul Ross
Paul Ross – he had the slipper
John James caused all the noise
and they're standing by the staffroom
with thirty other boys.

Five have lost their sarnies
five have lost their coats
five have found some sarnies
and five have found five coats
three have lost the hamster
two know where it's hid
and Emma's in the dustbin
and Sarah's thrown the lid.

It's another wet-time playtime
a day of all 'being in'
the game's called 'catch the culprit' –
and teachers never win!

Peter Dixon

Playtime — staying in

Sometimes it works –
A hand raised and a 'Please, Sir' . . .
You are amazed
That your,
'Please, I've got a cold, Sir,'
Touches him.
You stand alone
In a nearly silent classroom,
And the screams and shrieks
Drift to you from the tarmac
Where the hordes of savages
Fight it out
At playtime.

When they come bustling and shoving in
Sneering,
'Baby's got a cold,'
You are aware.
That you have missed something
Out there.

Gregory Harrison

It's not fair

One of us did it
but it wasn't me.

One of us said it
but it wasn't me.

I don't even know
who did it,
I don't even care
who said it.

One of us sitting here
knows who did it,
knows it wasn't me.

It was probably Michael
he's always talking when he shouldn't,
it might've been Tracey
she's always doing things she shouldn't.

But it wasn't me
and it's driving me mad
that I've got to stay here,
miss my playtime
just because
nobody dare say

it was me who did it
I said it, I did it.
Honest, it was me.

David Harmer

In summer

In summer at break we play cricket
But I really don't think I can stick it
For they roll up my pants
And make me take stance
And they use my thin legs as a wicket.

Philip C. Gross

Unfair

When we went over the park
Sunday mornings
To play football
we picked up sides.

Lizzie was our striker
because she had the best shot.

When the teachers
chose the school team
Marshy was our striker.

Lizzie wasn't allowed to play,
they said.

So she watched us lose, instead . . .

Michael Rosen

Picking teams

When we pick teams in the playground,
Whatever the game might be,
There's always somebody left till last
And usually it's me.

I stand there looking hopeful
And tapping myself on the chest,
But the captains pick the others first,
Starting, of course, with the best.

Maybe if teams were sometimes picked
Starting with the worst,
Once in his life a boy like me
Could end up being first!

Allan Ahlberg

SCRAPED CHALK SHRIEKS AND WHISPERS CREEP

I hear . . .

When I think of school
I hear
High shouts tossed
Like juggled balls in windy yards, and lost
In gutters, treetops, air.
And always, somewhere,
Piano-notes water-fall
And small sharp voices wail.
A monster-roar surges – 'Goal!'
The bell.
Then doors slam. There's the kick, scruff, stamp of shoes
Down corridors that trap and trail echoes.
Desk-tops thud with books, kit-bags,
A child's ghost screams as her chair's pushed back.
Laughter bubbles up and bursts.
Screech-owl whistles. Quick-fox quarrel-flares.
The voice barks 'QUIET!'
All sit. All wait.
Till scraped chalk shrieks
And whispers creep.
Cough. Ruler crack. Desk creak.
And furtive into the silence comes
A tiny mouse-scrabbling of pens.
Scamper. Stop. Scamper. Stop. Tiptoe.
And there, just outside the top window
As if it had never ceased to be
But only needed listening to
A scatter of birdsong, floating free.

Berlie Doherty

Learning

The stock cupboard's full of teachers
Sitting there drinking tea.
When I close the door I'm sure
They're all talking about me.

I saw my name on the blackboard
Three times it was underlined.
Though I rub it off each evening
It's back next day I find.

My books were in the head's study
He was tearing them apart.
Then he folded each page neatly
Into a paper dart.

I tried asking my mother
But she was on detention.
My dad was doing his homework
His face showing the tension.

So I'm going to be a teacher
And carve lessons on desk lids,
Keeping all the answers locked in
My cupboard away from kids.

Dave Alton

Two-minute girl

(In some schools, two minutes before classes start, a Two-Minute Girl or Boy pokes his or her head round the Staffroom door and warns the teachers to Get Ready.)

I'm the Two-Minute Girl
I'm about the size of a briefcase
I have bunches done up with barbed wire
And Count Dracula pointy teeth

I'm the Two-Minute Girl
I'm as sweet as syrup pudding on the surface
But I'm as wicked as stinging nettles underneath

Two minutes early or two minutes late
I stick my head round the Staffroom door
And sometimes I whisper like the ghost of a snake
(two minutes) and leave the teachers to snore

Yes I'm the Two-Minute Girl
I'm as cunning as cunning can be
With the driving brain of a diesel train
And the mischievousness of a flea

Oh I'm the Two-Minute Girl
I love to spread the Two-Minute Blues
Especially when I bellow TWO MINUTES
And a teacher pours the teapot all over his new suede shoes

Adrian Mitchell

Tables

Headmaster a come, mek has'e! Si '-down,
Amy! min' yuh bruck Jane collar-bone,
Tom! Tek yuh foot off o' de desk,
Sandra Wallace, mi know yuh vex
But beg yuh get up off o' Joseph head.
Tek de lizard off o' Sue neck, Ted!
Sue, mi dear, don' bawl so loud,
Thomas, yuh can tell mi why yuh a put de toad
Ena Elvira sandwich bag?
An, Jim, why yuh a do wid dah bull frog?
Tek i' off mi table! Yuh mad?
Mi know yuh chair small, May, but it no dat bad
Dat yuh haffe siddung pon de floor!
Jim, don' squeeze de frog unda de door,
Put i' through de window – no, no, Les!
Mi know yuh hungry, but Mary yeas
Won' full yuh up, so spit it out.
Now go wash de blood outa yuh mout.
Hortense, tek Mary to de nurse.
Nick, tek yuh han out o' Mary purse!
Ah wonda a who tell all o' yuh
Sey dat dis class-room is a zoo?
Si-down, Headmaster comin' through de door!
'Two ones are two, two twos are four.'

Valerie Bloom

Mr Cartwright's counting rhyme

One, two
You, boy, yes I'm talking to you

three, four
I've wiped the floor

five, six
with others of your kind. Your tricks

seven, eight
come centuries too late

nine, ten
for experienced men

eleven, twelve
like myself

thirteen, fourteen
so just be careful to be more seen

fifteen, sixteen
than heard, or preferably not seen

seventeen, eighteen
at all. Or you could stop baiting

nineteen, twenty
and pity me.

John Mole

Teachers

Don't scrape chairs, and don't be late
Play with doors, or swing the gate
Don't make noises,
Don't drop food,
Whistling's silly,
Raspberries rude . . .
Never fiddle,
Please don't shout
Never let your tongue poke out,
Don't lose pencils
Bend books back
Lose your plimsoles
(or plastic mac.)
Use your hankie
(not your cuff)
Never push and don't be rough
Mind the infants
Be polite
Watch the grass
And never fight
Keep off gardens
Don't pick flowers
Read this poem
 . . . BUT DON'T TAKE HOURS!!

Peter Dixon

Daydreamer

'Aljenard, Winston, Frederick,
Spencer, wha ya look out the winda sa?'
'Me alook pun the nice green grass!'
'But why do you look apun the nice green grass?'
'Me na no!'

'Aljenard, Winston, Frederick Spencer,
wha are ya look out the winda sa?'
'Me alook pun the bright blue sky!'
'But why do you look apun the bright blue sky?'
'Me na no!'

'Aljenard, Winston, Frederick,
Spencer, wha are ya look out the winda sa?'
'Me alook pun the hummin burd!'
'But why do you look apun the hummin burd?'
'Me na no!'

'Aljenard, Winston, Frederick,
Spencer, what are you look out the winda sa?'
'Me alook apun the glistening sun!'
'But why you look apun the glistening sun?'
'Me na no!'

'Aljenard, Winston, Frederick,
Spencer, wha are you look out the winda sa?'
'Me a try to feel the nice warm eir!'
'But why do you try to feel the nice warm eir?'

'Cause me a daydreamer!'

David Durham

The colour of my dreams

I'm a really rotten reader
the worst in all the class,
the sort of rotten reader
that makes you want to laugh.

I'm last in all the readin' tests,
my score's not on the page
and when I read to teacher
she gets in such a rage.

She says I cannot form my words
she says I can't build up
and that I don't know phonics
– and don't know c-a-t from k-u-p.

They say that I'm dyxlectic
(that's a word they've just found out)
but when I get some plasticine
I know what that's about.

I make these scary monsters
I draw these secret lands
and get my hair all sticky
and paint on all me hands.

I make these super models,
I build these smashing towers
that reach up to the ceiling
– and take me hours and hours.

I paint these lovely pictures
in thick green drippy paint
that gets all on the carpet –
and makes the cleaners faint.

I build great magic forests
weave bushes out of string
and paint pink panderellos
and birds that really sing.

I play my world of real believe
I play it every day
and teachers stand and watch me
but don't know what to say.

They give me diagnostic tests,
they try out reading schemes,
but none of them will ever know
the colour of my dreams.

Peter Dixon

Confusion

Jean get licks in school today
For hitting Janet Hill
It was just after recess time
And class was playful still
Janet pull Jean ribbon off
And throw it on the ground
Jean got vex and cuff Janet
Same time Miss turn around
Miss didn't ask no questions
She just start beating Jean
Tomorrow Jean mother coming
to fix-up Miss McLean.

Odette Thomas

Bad habit

Picking things is fun,
that's why teachers don't like me
to pick just any old thing,
but prefer it when I pick things up
like books I didn't drop
or sweet papers in the playground.
Teachers have told me 'once and for all'
that they do not approve of me picking enjoyable things
like my nose,
flowers from other people's gardens,
wax from my ears
or scabs from my knees.
They say things like:
'If you pick that again your finger will drop off.'
The only picking teachers like doing
is PICKING ON ME!

Frank Flynn

The miscreant

Standing outside the door
I am
victim of judgement.
Staff go by
glancing
with an enquiring eye,
but nothing's said.
Closed as a clam
I wear my guilt
internally
and wonder: Why
should it be ME?

Others were awkward.
Others tried
a trick or two –
but they're inside,
safe and secure,
and blandly taught.
I was the fellow
who was caught.
I was the chap
they fastened on:
'We've had enough
of you, my son.'

Drawn from the flock
as one who wouldn't
do what he should
(did what he shouldn't?)
I wait . . . and wait . . .
Each minute stretches
into an hour.
But no one fetches
the miscreant.
Whatever sin
it was,
why don't they
let me IN?

Jean Kenward

61

The bite

My grandmother, when she was little
was often bumptious.
In school, they used to punish her
(so she said)
by making her sit
with arms severely folded
and her starched pinafore
drawn up over her head.

Was it to force her penitence,
I wonder?
She wasn't sorry.
She bared her teeth to bite
and nicked a hole in the stuff.
She stuck her tongue out
through it, triumphant, wicked.

She was all right.

Jean Kenward

School inspection

'Well, what do you say?' the Inspector asked.
    'Just speak up! There's no need for thinking.'
'But if I don't think, how can I know
    What to say?' Mary answered him, blinking.

'Just blurt it out, girl! Say what you think,
    Without caring what words you may use.'
'But how can I speak,' said Mary, 'until
    I've decided which words I should choose?'

'Simply say what you mean,' the Inspector groaned,
    'Without all this absurd delay.'
'But how can I *tell* what I mean, Sir,
    Till I've heard what I've had to say!'

Raymond Wilson

YOU'RE STANDING ON A STRAWBERRY

63

School dinners

The greater-spotted brown baked bean's
not quite the humble bird it seems;
it lurks beneath the soggy greens
                  waiting to get you.

The green unruly jumping pea
has no respect for you or me;
it's bound to land on miss's knee
                  and she'll get you.

The brown-backed flying liverslug
is little better than a thug;
you think you're safe – don't be too smug
                  he'll get you.

The quiet skulking greasychip
looks innocent – that's just his trick;
eat thirds or fourths and you'll be sick
                  he'll get you.

The many-fingered crumb-y fish
looks friendly, as you might well wish;
but leave him lying on your dish
                  he'll get you.

Judith Nicholls

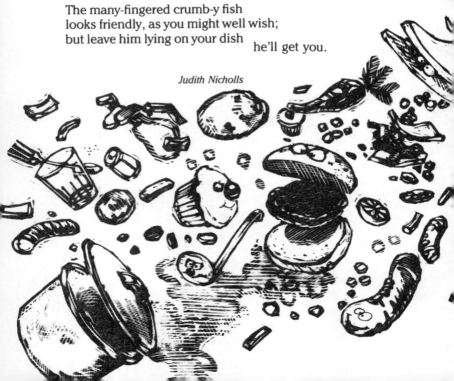

School dinner rhyme

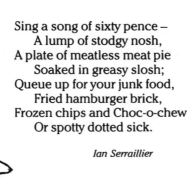

Sing a song of sixty pence –
    A lump of stodgy nosh,
A plate of meatless meat pie
    Soaked in greasy slosh;
Queue up for your junk food,
    Fried hamburger brick,
Frozen chips and Choc-o-chew
    Or spotty dotted sick.

Ian Serraillier

School dinner

'Dinning room' I should call it,
Not 'dining room'.
Someone opposite
Opens and shuts his mouth
Without your hearing a word he says,
Like the telly with sound switched off.

Strange, though, how everyone hears
The shout of 'Seconds'
And those who insulted the food
With names I won't repeat
Push for a place in the queue
And groan to hear the ladle
Scrape with an empty sound in the tray.

Dinner ladies wheel up pudding plates
Warm from the dishwasher still.

The second dinner sitting,
Bouncing their footballs,
Begin to arrive outside.

My empty plate stares up at me
To prove to me I couldn't possibly
Still be hungry.

Stanley Cook

You're standing on a strawberry

You're standing on a strawberry,
I heard the teacher say,
It was an end-of-term school dinner,
and we'd had strawberries that day;
You're standing on a strawberry,
and it isn't very good,
to put your great big feet,
in what's left of someone's pud!

You're sitting on a sausage,
and you're making such a mess,
that when you go home tonight
your mum will never guess,
what on earth you have been up to
to get in such a state;
It really is much better
to keep your dinner on a plate.

You've got your elbow in the custard
and it's soaking up your sleeve,
and such a mess you're making
no human could believe,
that one little bowl of custard
could go so very far,
and I promise you, my lad,
you'll get a belting from your ma.

You're slurping up the soup,
and you're spilling half your peas,
and there's a pencil and a ball-pen
embedded in the cheese.
Someone's dropped a plastic-spider
into the orange juice,
and teacher shouts for silence,
but it isn't any use.

It's just another dinner-time,
and it's very nearly done;
The battle of the servers,
has been fought, and lost, and won;
You scatter to the playground,
where you run so wild and free,
Whilst the teachers, in the staffroom,
have a quiet cup of tea.

John Cunliffe

S ausages, carrots
C ooked to a treat
H am, haslet, haggis
O r simple minced meat;
O ctopus, frogspawn, delicious to eat.
L et me go home to dinner, please miss!
D ainty brown rissoles peep from the gravy
I nteresting visitors peer from the peas
N ever say no to a wriggling wet noodle
N ot when it floats in tomato-red seas;
E veryone loves lumpy custard and gristle
R ace you for seconds, no cheating now, please!
S ee you later – I'm off to the chippy!

Judith Nicholls

67

NEVER SAY BOO!
TO A MOUSE

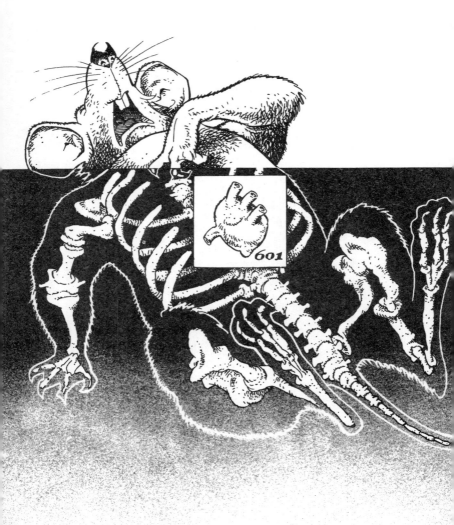

Never say boo! to a mouse

Sometimes at school you learn something useful,
Today we found out things about heart-
beats, like the hearts of young animals,
beat faster than the hearts of old animals,
or that big animals have a slower heart
beat than smaller animals.
An elephant's heart at rest
beats at twenty-five to fifty
times in a minute
whereas the heart of a mouse
beats at five hundred to six hundred and fifty
times in a minute.
At the end of the lesson
Mr Leather caught Gordon Grundy
reading a Spiderman comic
under the table. He asked Gordon
what he had learned about the heart
beats of elephants and mice.
Looking puzzled Gordon scratched
his head and picked his nose,
then he gave a relieved smile and said,
'You should never say BOO! to mice
They die of fright very easily.'

Frank Flynn

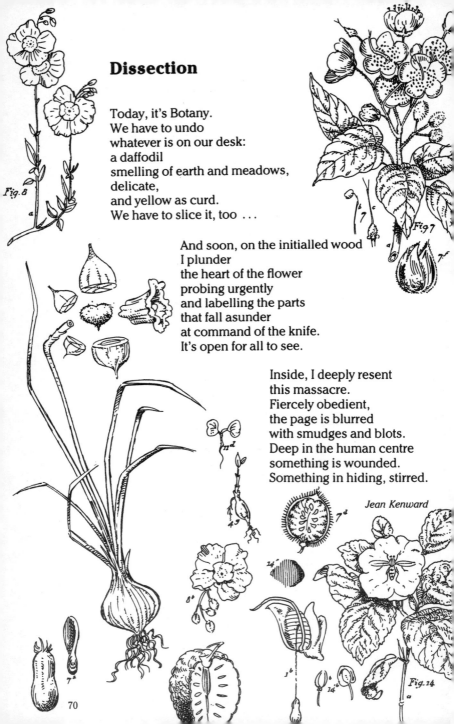

Dissection

Today, it's Botany.
We have to undo
whatever is on our desk:
a daffodil
smelling of earth and meadows,
delicate,
and yellow as curd.
We have to slice it, too ...

And soon, on the initialled wood
I plunder
the heart of the flower
probing urgently
and labelling the parts
that fall asunder
at command of the knife.
It's open for all to see.

Inside, I deeply resent
this massacre.
Fiercely obedient,
the page is blurred
with smudges and blots.
Deep in the human centre
something is wounded.
Something in hiding, stirred.

Jean Kenward

70

My teacher taught me how to see

My teacher taught me how to see
The lump within the daffodil's throat;
To look in clouds for the camel
And the bounding back of the stoat.

John Kitching

The reserve

School is a kind of nature reserve
Where gerbils can sleep undisturbed
And tadpoles have a better chance
Of growing up than in the wild.

Where else would tropical fish
Have it warm in the middle of winter
On a scientific diet
In tanks with all mod cons?

Where else would spiders be brought
With loving care from egg to web,
Mice have a cat-free home
And insects bird-free air?

And as for the teachers: do you remember
That man who stayed a term
Who taught us sitting cross-legged
on his desk like a guru?

How kind we always were to him!
How kind we always are to them!

Stanley Cook

The blackboard

Five foot by five foot
(The smalls have measured it).
Smooth black surface
(Wiped by a small after every class).
Five different colours of chalk
And a class of twenty-five smalls,
One big.

Does the big break up the chalk
Into twenty-five or twenty-six
And invite the smalls to make
A firework show of colours
Shapes and words
Starting on the blackboard
But soon overflowing
   All over the room
      All over the school
         All over the town
            All over the country
               All over the world?

        No.

The big looks at the textbook
Which was written by a big
And published by a firm of bigs.
The textbook says
The names and dates of Nelson's battles.
So the big writes, in white,
Upon the black of the blackboard,
The names and dates of Nelson's battles.
The smalls copy into their books
The names and dates of Nelson's battles.

      Nelson was a big
Who died fighting for freedom or something.

Adrian Mitchell

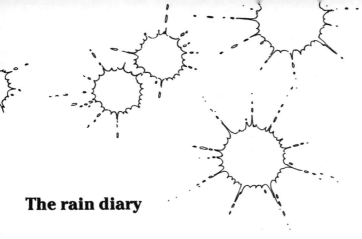

The rain diary

For my geography project, I would keep a rain diary, a record starting on 1st January of the days that year when it rained and approximately how much.

On 1st January there was no rain. On 2nd January there was no rain. It did not rain on 3rd or 4th either. Would I go back to Littlemere Road School on 8th January with nothing to show? Only blank pages with the date in blue-black italic and the expectation of punishment?

Amanda kept a sunshine diary. The sun shone all the time that New Year, every day was like the legendary 1st January 1942. I saw long shadows of bare trees in Amanda's garden revolving on the stiff white grass as the sun crawled low and bright round the Warwickshire sky. Amanda, day by day, logged her hours of sunshine in duffle coat and mittens, putting out her tongue to warm her finger-tips.

Tiny planes inched over the blue from the aerodrome leaving lacy strips of vapour which crumbled into strung-out blurs. There was no rain on 5th, 6th or 7th. I gained a sense of what life in general would be like.

On 8th January I stood at 8.55 a.m. on the worn stone step of the school with my blank diary – and raindrops fell. But I had no time to write anything down, the bell was pounding in the campanile and we could not be late. So I opened my rain diary and let the rain fall into it, stain it and crinkle it, as the others ran past me into school.

To which rain I added my own joyful tears, knowing that Amanda might have statistics but I had a concrete event.

Alan Brownjohn

Function machine

IN

NITWIT
LAZYBONES
DIMWIT
DUMB

WORDSPELL
TABLETEST
WRITE-A-LOT
SUM

NUMBSKULL
LIE-A-BED
WOOLLYHEAD
FOOL

BRAINFUL
EGGHEAD
WORK + SWEAT

SCHOOL!

OUT

(GENIUS)

Judith Nicholls

Forget it!

'The great trouble,' he said, 'with me
Is my short-term memory.
Between one fleeting hour and another
I quite forget this, that and the other.'

'I'm sure,' I said, 'you exaggerate.
But how long have you been in this state?'
'Which state?' – 'Not remembering, you know.'
'Who?' 'You.' *'Me!'* he said. 'Who told you so?'

Raymond Wilson

Computer time

I ... plod ... my ... way ...
Through ... Wordwise ...
I ... slowly ... poke ... the ... keys
I ... watch ... the ... text ...
Upon ... the ... screen ...
It ... only ... seems ... to ... tease ...
It's ... dull ... and ... pretty ... lonely ...
And ... hard ... upon ... this chair ...
I'd ... rather ... sit ... on ... teachers' ... knees ...
And ... have ... them ... stroke ... my ... hair ...
When reading ... tales of ... dragons,
Castles, witches ... princes fair
And boiling oil ... and stormy seas,
Treasures dangerous and rare
Where all is magic, frightening
But safe. I ... just ... don't ... care ...
To ... slowly ... prod ... away ... my ...days ...
Unwisely ... on ... these ... Wordwise ... keys.

John Kitching

BEWARE OF THE HISTORY TEACHER

Lesson in history

Beware of the history teacher,
Cause of many a pupil's sorrow,
Though he drones on about the past
His homework is due in tomorrow.

Dave Alton

I love to do my homework

I love to do my homework,
It makes me feel so good.
I love to do exactly
As my teacher says I should.

I love to do my homework,
I never miss a day,
I even love the men in white
Who are taking me away.

Anon

The song of the homeworkers

To be read or chanted with increasing velocity.

Homework moanwork
Cross it out and groan work
Homework neatwork
Keeps you off the streetwork
Homework moanwork
Cross it out and groanwork
Homework roughwork
When you've had about enoughwork
Homework moanwork
Cross it out and groanwork
Homework dronework
Do it on your ownwork
Homework moanwork
Cross it out and groanwork
Homework gloomwork
Gaze around the roomwork
Homework moanwork
Cross it out and groanwork
Homework guesswork
Book is in a messwork
Homework moanwork
Cross it out and groanwork
Homework rushwork
Do it on the buswork
Homework moanwork
Cross it out and groanwork
Homework hatework
Hand your book in latework
Homework moanwork
Cross it out and groan groan GROANWORK!

Trevor Millum

Where's your homework?

As soon as I got home last night, Sir
I finished off my English homework first.
Put it on the kitchen table but my baby sister
found it. Chewed it and slavered all over it, Sir.
So I took it into the bath to check it through
like you asked us to do, Sir.
But reaching for the sponge
I dropped it in the bath.
It was so soggy that
I had to put the hair drier on it.
I burnt it to a crisp. Bone dry the paper was, Sir.
So I had a brainwave. I smeared Suntan lotion
on it to soften it up.
Left it for ten minutes
and the pages started to turn brown.

This morning I looked inside
and all the writing was smudged, Sir.
Could I have a new exercise book, please?

David Jackson

The lesson

A poem that raises the question:
Should there be capital punishment in schools?

Chaos ruled OK in the classroom
as bravely the teacher walked in
the hooligans ignored him
his voice was lost in the din

'The theme for today is violence
and homework will be set
I'm going to teach you a lesson
one that you'll never forget'

He picked on a boy who was shouting
and throttled him then and there
then garrotted the girl behind him
(the one with grotty hair)

Then sword in hand he hacked his way
between the chattering rows
'First come, first severed' he declared
'fingers, feet, or toes'

He threw the sword at a latecomer
it struck with deadly aim
then pulling out a shotgun
he continued with his game

The first blast cleared the backrow
(where those who skive hang out)
they collapsed like rubber dinghies
when the plug's pulled out

'Please may I leave the room sir?'
a trembling vandal enquired
'Of course you may' said teacher
put the gun to his temple and fired

The head popped a head round the doorway
to see why a din was being made
nodded understandingly
then tossed in a grenade

And when the ammo was well spent
with blood on every chair
Silence shuffled forward
with its hands up in the air

The teacher surveyed the carnage
the dying and the dead
He waggled a finger severely
'Now let that be a lesson' he said

                    Roger McGough

O's

A little boy called Robert Rose,
Whenever reading verse or prose
Would often colour in the O's.
He used a pencil for the job
And made each O an odious blob.

Unhappily for Robert Rose,
He caught a strange disease
Where O's appeared between his toes
And then behind his knees.

His elbow, throat and then his nose
Were slowly overgrown with O's,
Then suddenly, oh woe, alack!
Those ovals went completely black.

He died of course, which only shows
You shouldn't mess around with O's!

Doug Macleod

A pencil case

'So you say your school's been burgled,'
the policeman scratched his face,
'And there's nothing left to write with
— this looks like a pencil case.'

John Rice

Writing and sums

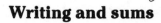

When the teacher asks us to write,
The words dance in my head,
Weaving neat patterns,
Gliding into their places,
Before flowing down my pencil
In an orderly procession.
But . . .
When the teacher tells me to do sums,
The figures fly round my head,
Fluttering like birds
Trapped behind glass,
Before tumbling down my pencil
In frightened confusion.

Derek Stuart

The thin prison

Hold the pen close to your ear.
Listen – can you hear them?
Words burning as a flame,
Words glittering like a tear,

Locked, all locked in the slim pen.
They are crying for freedom.
And you can release them,
Set them running from prison.

Himalayas, balloons, Captain Cook,
Kites, red bricks, London Town,
Sequins, cricket bats, large brown
Boots, lions and lemonade – look,

I've just let them out!
Pick up your pen, and start,
Think of the things you know – then
Let the words dance from your pen.

Leslie Norris

New notebook

Lines
in a new notebook
run, even and fine,
like telephone wires
across a snowy landscape.

With wet, black strokes
the alphabet settles between them,
comfortable as a flock of crows.

Judith Thurman

The exercise book

The world is going to be sorry one day
That I threw this exercise book away,
Unless by a miracle it survives
The rubbish tip or stokehole fires.

You know how the monks in the Middle Ages
Used to fill the margins of their pages
With drawings of what their life was like –
When they weren't ploughing they were reaping,
When they weren't sowing they were threshing.
When they weren't hunting they were fishing
And those were certainly hard-working times.

I did the same with the margins of mine
And every page has drawings from life –
That brilliant group and the greatest team
That should win this, that and then some,
The names of the great and the latest hair styles,
The people I hate and the people I like.

How can HE say
This book looks as if
The rats have been at it?

Stanley Cook

Teacher said . . .

You can use
    mumbled and muttered,
    groaned, grumbled and uttered
    professed, droned or stuttered
             . . . but *don't* use SAID!

You can use
    rant or recite
    yell, yodel or snort
    bellow, murmur or moan
    you can grunt or just groan
             . . . but *don't* use SAID!

You can
    hum, howl and hail
    scream, screech, shriek or bawl
    squeak, snivel or squeal
    with a blood-curdling wail
             . . . but *don't* use SAID!

             . . . SAID my teacher.

Judith Nicholls

I am a full stop

I am a full stop.
At my command,
sentences halt.
At its peril,
a letter which follows me
forgets it should be a capital.
I place myself between words.
I create meaning.
When children ignore me,
I cause confusion.
I am a full stop.
Learn to control *me*
and the whole written world
is yours.

Derek Stuart

Comparisons

Similes are as hard as hell,
Metaphors are a swine!
'Be original,' the teacher says,
He doesn't have a brain like mine!

All last night, I worked like a slave,
Over hot coals I toiled,
Only to find at every turn
My efforts all were foiled.

If ever I am lucky enough
To find the images I'm seeking,
I'm sure I would be top of the class
– comparatively speaking!

Ray Mather

Summing up

A poet came to our school
to earn his daily bread,
a real live poet
with words in his head.
He told us to write a poem
before the lunchtime bell.
We said that we would,
if he would as well.
Some of ours were rather good,
but his face was rather red
because he couldn't do one –
his words were prisoners in his head.
He said he hadn't been inspired –
that's just like me with sums:
I sit and stare at numbers,
but inspiration never comes.

Nigel Gray

My teacher said
'Write a poem about fossils'

Backbones are good.

I have got a backbone.
A fossil hasn't got a backbone.
Everybody has got a backbone.
It goes from the bottom of your back
up to your head.
You can feel the bumps
and when someone goes swimming
in their swimming trunks then you can
see the bumps of their backbone
especially if they bend over to go down
the water slide, there's too many bumps to count.
I got the bumps on my birthday
and Sarah let go of my arm and
I nearly fell on my head.
I can't stand Sarah now.
She nearly made me fall on my head.
Our school has got a head.
He says our teachers are all backbones
of the school.
None of us know what he is talking about
when he says our teachers are all backbones.
My dad says teachers are spineless.
I don't think they are cause if they were
spineless it means that they don't have
backbones, right?
And if they don't have backbones
then they'd just flop over like
a dead cat trying to stand up.

Our cat has got a backbone.
It sleeps on top of the TV
and when my dad comes in he shouts
at it to get off because it hangs
its tail over the front of the screen
and he wants to see the news properly.
It wakes up with a fright and stretches
its front legs first, then yawns
with its white teeth nearly biting its own tongue.
Then it bends its backbone so much
that the whole cat looks just like
a black coathanger hook.
My dad shouts again and it gets straight.

I don't know any words that rhyme with backbone.
I don't know if a camel has got a backbone.
If it has it must have got broken
when a bridge fell on it.
The end – I think.
Well I don't know what else I can say
about a fossil except that once
my teacher got a big blood blister
when she accidentally slammed the desk lid
on her thumb when she was annoyed
with Anthony Warren.
She kept us all in at break for laughing.
Then she said 'Right, just for your cheek
you can all write a poem about fossils
for homework!'

John Rice

Extra-curricular activity

Writing a poem to be buried in a time capsule

Well, now, I hardly know just how I should begin.
In the first place, whom, exactly,
am I supposed to be addressing? Should I call you
Mr, Mrs, Miss or Ms? B.A.? M.A.? Or even Professor, Ph.D?
Or are you perhaps a 'Sir' this or a 'Lady' that?
(Highly unlikely, now I come to think of it —
the aristocracy already seems a dying race.)

Can you read English? I hope so. Can you even read?
The way things are going these days, poetry and books
may soon be things of the past. (What? No more comics?)
— Are you more or less like me? Or barely human? Invader
from outermost space, come at last to colonize our earth (if
there's anything left of it) with robot armies of right-wing kids?
(Today's lot are pretty spaced-out, on totalitarian trips.)

O.K. then, this is it. Whoever you are, this is my poem
that our English teacher, Sneakers, gave us to write for
    homework
on this far-out time capsule idea. At least forty lines!
(Personally, I think it's pretty weird. Whatever next?)
Then our class are going to take their poems, signed and
    dated,
after school next Monday, after they've been marked,
    corrected and
re-written in our best handwriting, to bury them on the Downs

in this really neat time capsule they've made in Metalwork.
But what a crazy notion! I ask you, whoever you are,
who cares? What does it matter? And what's in it for me?
I can tell you the poems are sure to be a load of rubbish
like this one . . .
                — Or is it? I've only just realized I'm writing it
as if I fully expected it to be read in a hundred years' time
by you, mate, wherever, whoever or whatever you are. Good
    grief!

James Kirkup

Poem to be buried in a time capsule

My poem is in itself
a kind of time capsule.
It contains my essence,
my native speech,
my choice of words,
my thought, my laughter
and my very breath.

You can swallow it
like a vitamin pill —
one that you absorb
through eyes and ears,
until your own lungs,
throat, tongue and lips
reconstitute its voice.

Through its lines you hear
my own voice speaking
across the centuries.
Though I have long been dead,
this poem is a living thing
from secret sources
that are living still.

Be careful as you
unearth my mystery; and
unwind my age-old wrappings
tenderly, with understanding
of my fragility, that hides
an unsuspected toughness
preserving precious seeds.

— Because a time capsule poem
is also a kind of time bomb
whose delayed-action meanings
can only be safely defused
by those who learn to read
between the lines. — Otherwise
I self-destruct! So mind what you do.

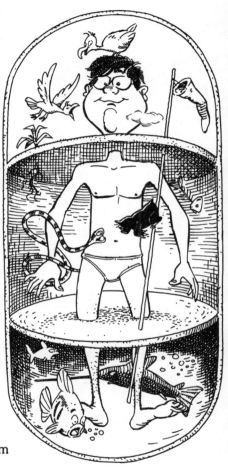

James Kirkup

Exams

Exams aren't fun.
You don't get many people
going to exams for their holidays.

They don't show exam highlights
on Match of the Day,
there's no Exam of the Month competition
or action replays.

You can't chew or drink exams
and when you put them on
they're really dull and dated.

No, exams aren't cheerful.
Imagine taking an exam to the disco,
who'd do that?

Or paying to see one dance and sing
at an end-of-the-pier show?

You'd think my teachers
would agree with me, see
the reason in what I'm saying.

If exams had been here years ago
they'd all have been hanged
for sleep stealing.

David Harmer

The music examiner

The music examiner stood
As I played as well as I could
But, shaking his head
'An oboe,' he said
'Is an ill-wind that no one blows good.'

Philip C. Gross

Dear Mr Examiner

Thank you so much for your questions
I've read them most carefully through
But there isn't a single one of them
That I know the answer to.

I've written my name as instructed
Put the year, the month and the day
But after I'd finished doing that
I had nothing further to say.

So I thought I'd write you a letter
Fairly informally
About what I can see from my desk here
And what it's like to be me.

Mandy has written ten pages
But it's probably frightful guff
And Angela Smythe is copying
The answers off her cuff.

Miss Quinlan is marking our homework
The clock keeps ticking away
I suppose for anyone outside
It's just another day.

There'll be mothers going on errands
Grandmothers sipping tea
Unemployed men doing crosswords
or watching 'Crown Court' on TV.

The rain has finally stopped here
The sun has started to shine
And in a back garden in Sefton Drive
A housewife hangs shirts on a line.

A class files past to play tennis
The cathedral clock has just pealed
A mower chugs backwards and forwards
Up on the hockey field.

Miss Quinlan's just read what I've written
Her face is an absolute mask
Before she collects the papers in
I've a sort of favour to ask.

I thought your questions were lovely
I've only myself to blame
But couldn't you give me some marks
For writing the date and my name.

Gareth Owen

Trips

For our school trip this term
we're going to Mars.

It's £1.50.
We're taking sandwiches
and a flask.

We might be back late at night
but as long as the driver gets it right
we won't splash down off Scarborough.

I'd rather go to the zoo.
There isn't much to do on Mars.

Next term
We're going to the sun.

It's £3.00.
We're taking swimming trunks
and dark glasses.

We'll be camping overnight
and as long as the driver gets it right
we won't splash down off Scarborough.

I'd rather go to the zoo.
I've seen the sun before.

Ian McMillan and Martyn Wiley

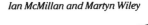

A visit to the zoo

Now then children, form a queue
Let me count you going through
27, 29; Daphne darling, stay in line
30, 31 & 2; Sandra, where's your other shoe?
Leave your knickers Pam my pet
Take them *off* then if they're wet!
Hands up those who need the loo
Off you go then. Follow Prue.
Wendy! Mandy! NOT IN THERE!!
That's the GENTS you dozy pair.
Donna dear, you can't stroke that
That's no ordinary cat.
Blow your nose Ann, don't just sniff.
Sue your hat is on skew-whiff.
No, the parrot doesn't swear
You provoke him if you dare.
Hilary! For heaven's sake
Who pushed Cathy in the lake?
O-oh Yvonne, my tiny friend
Elephants eat at the *other* end.
Come along now. Time for lunch
Settle down you noisy bunch.
Dilys, don't you want to eat?
Child! You're whiter than a sheet!
What's that darling, Abigail's
Got her head stuck in the rails!
Fetch the keeper someone. Quick!
(Rotten kids, they make me sick)
Keeper, *don't* just stand and grin
Open a cage and put me in!

J. J. Webster

London trip

A poem dedicated to teachers and other grown-ups who take children to London.

When we went up to London
The coach was blue and white.
We went all round the Tower
And we saw just every sight.
We visited the V & A
We visited the zoo
And went and watched the Palace Guards
And saw things soldiers do.

When we went up to London
My sandwiches were spam
And Billy Mills had egg and cheese
And 'arny Whitehouse ham.
Johnny Jones had bread and paste
And Maggie Jones had pork
. . . and when we went to London
our teacher made us WALK!

We walked all round Trafalgar Square,
We walked all round St. Paul's
And whispered things that didn't work
On whispering gallery walls.

When we went to London
The top came off my drink
And ran all down my trousers –
And made a nasty stink . . .
It got all on the coach seats
It trickled on the floor
It trickled on Miss Gardner's bag
And trickled through the door . . .

The Science Museum was not too bad –
The toilets there were fun,
We played a game called pull the chain
– and slam the door – and run.
We chased around the old steam trains,
We pulled those pulley things –
And Martin Knight – he pulled one off
And snapped those bits with springs.

The Albert Hall was really bad,
The Tate was boring too . . .
And that was when poor Enid White
Spilt all her curried stew.
. . . The man in there got really cross
He shouted REALLY LOUD
And everyone came running round and
Formed a great big crowd.

Miss Gardner . . . well . . .
She sees this crowd,
And smells the curried stew,
And guesses that it's Enid White,
The way that teachers do –
And so – you see – we had to go
(though we'd wiped the pictures clean),
But the journey on the bus back home
Was the best that's ever been!
Norman had a pigeon
He'd got in Trafalgar Square
And he said it had a broken wing,
'til it flew up in the air!
It flew all round the driver's cab
It landed in his hair!
And made him wind the window down,
And curse, and yell, and swear.

Miss Gardner – she got really cross,
And made poor Norman cry,
He really thought the bird was hurt
    and couldn't hardly fly.
And then we got the punctures.
We got three in a row,
And stuck in Blackwell Tunnel,
When the engine wouldn't go.
We had four smashing breakdowns,
The driver lost his way
We were five hours late returning
From a really super day!!

Three cheers for Miss Gardner and our driver,

Hip . . . Hip . . . . !!!!!!!!!

Peter Dixon

A flash of moonlight on a sunny afternoon

'REDUCED RATES FOR PARTIES,' the sign promised
so as part of the school outing we paid
for an hour long trip around the bay,
with some fishing included in the price.

Spaced evenly around the edge of the boat
twelve children and a teacher sit,
wrinkling their noses at the smell
of diesel oil and dead fish
that rises from the well of the boat.
As the *Anna* butts out into the swell
the waving figure of the headmistress
shrinks on the harbour wall.

Spray tangs face and lips,
the children soon become thirsty and bored,
some even start to feel sick.
As a distraction hand lines
baited with ragged bits of fish that hang
from the bronzed hooks like tattered flags,
are thrown over the side.

The eager anticipation of the children
glides gull-like around the boat
rising to a high pitched squeal of triumph
as the captain takes a line from the shaking hands
of a blonde girl in a red swimming costume,
and hauls it in with the calm competence
of one who is bored by a task done
too many times before.

In a single smooth movement
he flips a flash of moonlight
into a large, battered, plastic bucket.
The class crowd around to watch
as a slender mackerel arcs for breath.
Its body a bridge between death and life
the fish struggles hard and dies slowly.

The children lose interest long before an end
that is signalled by the fish finally lying still,
blood oozing lightly from its gills,
the young are easily bored, even by death.

Back at the harbour the children race away
towards promised ice creams and coke,
unwanted the fish is left as bait
for the next trip around the bay.

Frank Flynn

School sports day

The flags are streaming in a sunny breeze —
blue, green, yellow, red and white
above the freshly-whitewashed running tracks
all round the grassy sports-ground. New-mown,
the field's lush edges still are starred
with buttercups and daisies, dandelion clocks.

Music plays. From time to time the starter's pistol explodes
whole colonies of rooks from leafy elms under whose
shade old boys and parents and the head cheer on the
last relay teams, the first heats of the sprints, while
(Ooh!) the pole-vaulter does a space walk from his pole,
the high-jumper bounces after a beautiful Fosbury flop.

Tea-urns hiss in the warm marquee. Coke bottles sweat.
Bright bunting drapes the plastic tablecloths
on which the paper plates of sandwiches and pies,
hot sausage rolls and sugar buns and home-made cakes
attract the orchard wasps — and hungry boys and girls
flushed with the final heats, the prize-giving's proud applause.

As the long day cools to evening, we wander, tired
and stiff, but glad it's over, down the country lanes,
accompanying relatives and friends to car-parks
or the village station and its cottage flower-beds.
— Then slowly back to school for evening prayers,
lights out, larks, laughter — and dreams of coming holidays.

James Kirkup

WHERE DO ALL THE TEACHERS GO?

Where do all the teachers go . . .?

Where do all the teachers go
when it's 4 o'clock?
Do they live in houses,
and do they wash their socks?
Do they wear pyjamas?
And do they watch TV?
And do they pick their noses
just like you and me?
Do they live with other people?
Have they mums and dads?
And were they ever children?
And were they ever bad?
Did they ever never spell right?
Did they ever make mistakes?
Or get put in the corner,
or pinch the chocolate cakes?

Did they ever lose their hymn books
did they ever leave their greens
or scribble on the desk top
or wear some dirty jeans?

I'll follow one back home one day
I'll find out what they do . . .

                    . . . and tell you in a poem

That they can read to you.

Peter Dixon

4 p.m.

Paint dry,
pens gone;
chalk dust
drifts down.

Pawns still,
knights wait;
kings sleep,
checkmate!

Books closed,
maths done;
ghosts stir
alone.

Judith Nicholls

Plodders

We homeward plod, our satchels full
Of books to make our evenings dull.
We homeward plod, our heads hung low,
Crammed full of facts One Ought to Know.

Tomorrow we will plod once more
To school, where we will stay till four,
Or thereabouts, for that is when,
With books, we'll homeward plod again.

Colin West

Going home

There were two ways of going home:
the tender
touch of the moss
upon the sun-blessed wall,
soft to my fingers,
squashy as marshmallow . . .
the hum of bees . . .
the warm, endearing call
of summer –
like a visitor who comes
and stays,
and still is welcome here,
and lingers.

Or that more desolate return
on lonely
days, when I was the last
to venture out
having been punished
for some misdemeanour.
There, by the corner,
she'd be waiting,
stout
and geared to harm:
a bully girl, enjoying
her ominous approach
to twist my arm.

I was too little, then,
to learn the wit
that might avoid encounter –
run away
or find my path home
by a new direction.
Fear kept me silent.
What was there to say?
Having inflicted pain, at last
she'd quit.
Released, my furtive sob repressed and private,
safe at my door,
I wouldn't mention it.

Jean Kenward

Swot

They pinch my bag
rip the strap off
stuff it with Stink Horn
leave it in the shower

throw pumps at me
call me 'Crab Eyes'
tie my legs together
roll me down the bank.

I told the form master once.
They took my rough book
wrote GRASS all over
in green felt tip.

It's not my fault
I'm good at maths
and don't like
a hard ball.

I didn't ask
for my father to be
a pacifist, and say
'Never fight'.

I know I'm rather
absentminded
and sometimes
don't hear the bell

I know I'm
a bit eccentric
and sometimes
chatter on like a kid

but when I'm happy
my time's not theirs
but the kind
clouds have, in the summer.

I'd like to leave,
live on an island –
on melons
and coconut scoop

do calculus
with my feet up,
ride elephant turtles
down to the sea.

Geoffrey Holloway

Homework

Who invented homework?
What is it all for?
I already do enough in class
Why give me any more?

When I get back home
I want to be free,
I just want to put my feet up
and watch a little TV.

I work hard all day,
And deserve a rest
If they give me so much to do
How can I do my best?

I've heard their excuses
And I think they're poor
'You need to study on your own.'
What on earth for?

My dad has a job
In an office all day.
If work was waiting for him at home,
I know what he would say!

There is just one thing
That might change my view
And that's if they paid us overtime!
Wouldn't that suit you, too?

Ray Mather

News break

Now why so loving, darling,
And why the sudden kiss?
You'd help me with some little jobs?
For goodness sake, what's this?

Your face is clean for once, dear.
Your clothes without a crease.
You saved your luncheon money?
Will wonders never cease?

No dropping of your school books,
No shrieking, childish treble.
Today you are a lamb, love,
Where yesterday a rebel.

But surely you're some stranger,
No rage or hullabaloo.
Come closer, let me, look, dear,
Can this be REALLY you?

Now were you struck by lightning
Or were you stunned at sport?
Ah . . . now I see the reason.
You've brought your school report!

Max Fatchen

Making the grade

I've never won a medal
at sports,
I've never been picked
for the choir,
I'm not good enough
for the school team,
I doubt if I'll pass
my cycling proficiency test.

I'm really not much good at anything.

But at night, just before
I drop off to sleep, I picture myself
winning the London Marathon,
singing the number one song on
Top of the Pops,
scoring the winning goal
and coming first into Paris
in the Tour de France cycle race.

I get so carried away I yell out 'YES!!'
and waken my big brother who moans
'Get back to sleep, you stupid pig.'

John Rice

Progress report

' . . . and you can't go
In that scruffy jacket either –
You'll look a proper fool.'
Mum and Dad getting ready to go
To the Progress Meeting
At school.
Dad says, 'Come to that,
Is that the dress you're going to wear?
Lean forward with that neckline
And your bellybutton's bare!'
They did get gone eventually,
Both suitably dressed in black,
Gone to a big session of talk
About me –
Behind my blooming back.

'He's really had an excellent term.
The work's been very demanding –
But in English, Maths, History, Geog . . .
In everything he's outstanding.
On the sports field too he's broken records –
Well, look at the trophies he's lifted . . .
And in Music he just plays everything,
He's really wonderfully gifted.'
'No weaknesses anywhere at all!' gasps Dad.
(Mum's looking over the moon).
'Absolutely none,' Sir firmly states,
'I'm sure he'll be Head Boy soon.
And meeting you both this evening,
Well, it's not difficult to see
Where your son's brilliance comes from . . .'
Says Mum (and Dad), 'From me!'

And that's where the dreaming ended.
'You've been asleep by the telly,' says Mum;
They were back from the Progress Meeting,
Both looking pretty glum.
'I had a bit of a dream . . .' I said.
'That's your problem,' said Dad,
'Dreaming instead of doing,
You need to shape yourself, my lad.
Your teacher says in English and Maths
Your marks are very low,
And in Geography, History and all that stuff –
Well, you just don't want to know.
No interest in Games or Music,' he says,
'None in Art or Drama –'
'Save the rest for the morning,' says Mum,
'By then you'll be feeling calmer.'

And I trailed off to bed
Heart heavy as lead,
Mind silently screaming,
'Better pack in the dreaming.'

Eric Finney

But I didn't

When I got out of bed this morning
I might have tripped and fallen down
The stairs, breaking my neck as I did so
But I didn't,
Going to school
The bus might have crashed
In the morning rain
But it didn't,
There might have been an earthquake
Causing the school to collapse
Before my maths test
But there wasn't,
Eating school dinner
The fish might easily have been poisoned
Leaving me feeling dead
Instead of just sick, as usual,
But it wasn't,
The sweet shop I visited after school
Might have been robbed by men
With sawn-off shotguns
Leaving me wounded
When I became a hero and tried to stop them
But it wasn't,
I might have disturbed a burglar
When I got home
Instead of my mum taking a nap
But I didn't,
Because I don't take chances
Nothing much happens to me
I'm careful never to walk on black lines
Between paving stones
And I always touch my nose and toes
Whenever I see an ambulance,
Being careful can be boring
Tomorrow I might start taking chances
But I won't.

Frank Flynn

SCHOOLDAYS
COME
IN SQUARES

Timetable

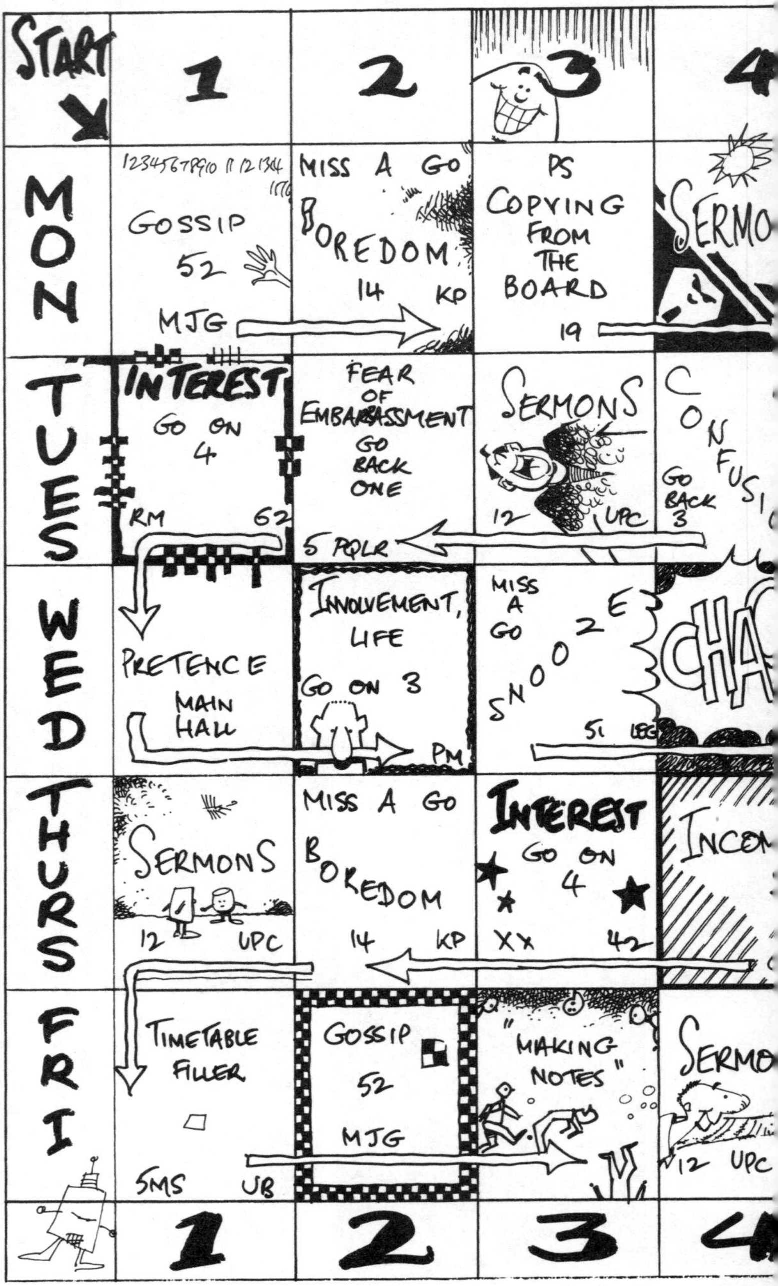

START
1
2
3
4
MON
TUES
WED
THURS
FRI
GOSSIP
52
MJG
MISS A GO
BOREDOM
14 KP
PS
COPYING FROM THE BOARD
19
SERMO
INTEREST
GO ON 4
RM 62
FEAR OF EMBARASSMENT
GO BACK ONE
5 PQLR
SERMONS
12 UPC
CONFUSI
GO BACK 3
PRETENCE
MAIN HALL
INVOLVEMENT, LIFE
GO ON 3
PM
MISS A GO
SNOOZE
51 LEG
CHA
SERMONS
12 UPC
MISS A GO
BOREDOM
14 KP
INTEREST
GO ON 4
XX 42
INCOM
TIMETABLE FILLER
SMS UB
GOSSIP
52
MJG
"MAKING NOTES"
SERMO
12 UPC
1
2
3
4

Trevor Millum

Squares

Schooldays come in squares, four in the morning,
Three in the afternoon, five times over
Every week, most weeks of the year,
For years. Schools and classrooms come in squares:
You sit in your desks knitted in rows.
But holidays unwind wherever you like;
You can tangle your time or tie it in knots,
Like a cat unravelling wool;
Use your toe, not a thermometer,
To take the water's temperature;
See the fish you saw in a diagram
Swimming in the stream;
And show how bicycles work
While sitting in the saddle:
All until another term
Knits it into squares again.

Stanley Cook

My long scarf

On the first day back in September
the year stretches out like a scarf.

I wrap it around me
until well after Christmas.

The further through the year I go
the more the scarf unravels,

until the very last day of school
when all that's left is a pile of wool.

Ian McMillan and Martyn Wiley

Winter term

Headmasters and headmistresses
Have chopped the year in three:
We've autumn, spring and summer terms,
But where can winter be?

What have they done with winter, do
They think they're being kind
In making us feel winter is
A figment of the mind?

It seems that winter's been condensed
To just two weeks or three,
Renamed the Christmas holiday –
That's how it seems to me.

Colin West

A snowy day at school

Five Haiku

Overnight, the snow
has turned into one long slope
our five schoolyard steps.

No one can sit on
the playground swings, buried deep
under drifts of snow.

In still-falling snow
perching crows shake trees of flakes
in still-falling snow.

Classroom radiant
with snowlight. Your face reflects
each slow-turning page.

The whole classroom seems
to start silently rising
in still-falling snow.

James Kirkup

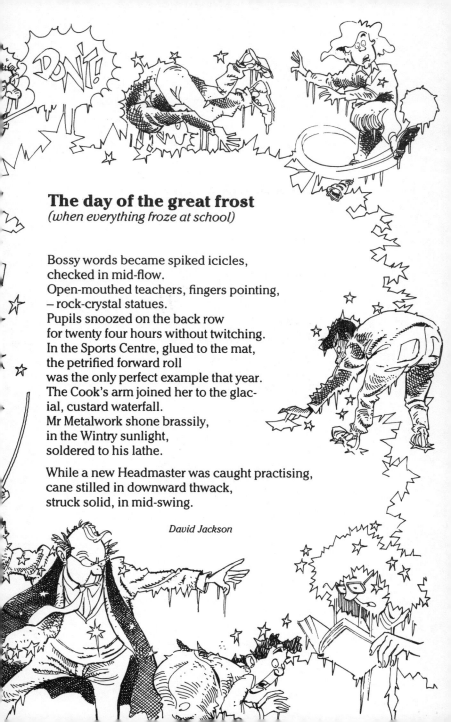

The day of the great frost
(when everything froze at school)

Bossy words became spiked icicles,
checked in mid-flow.
Open-mouthed teachers, fingers pointing,
– rock-crystal statues.
Pupils snoozed on the back row
for twenty four hours without twitching.
In the Sports Centre, glued to the mat,
the petrified forward roll
was the only perfect example that year.
The Cook's arm joined her to the glac-
ial, custard waterfall.
Mr Metalwork shone brassily,
in the Wintry sunlight,
soldered to his lathe.

While a new Headmaster was caught practising,
cane stilled in downward thwack,
struck solid, in mid-swing.

David Jackson

The school caretaker

In the corner of the playground
Down dark and slimy stairs,
Lived a monster with a big nose
Full of curly hairs.

He had a bunch of keyrings
Carved out of little boys,
He confiscated comics
And all our favourite toys.

He wore a greasy uniform,
Looked like an undertaker,
More scary than a horror film,
He was the school caretaker.

I left the school some years ago;
Saw him again the other day.
He looked rather sad and old
Shuffling on his way.

It's funny when you grow up
How grown-ups start growing down,
And the snarls upon their faces
Are no more than a frown.

In the corner of the playground
Down dark and slimy stairs,
Sits a lonely little man
With a nose full of curly hairs.

Brian Patten

The ghost

I am the Ghost of School.
I lie
in secret places,
silently.
A mist of chalk dust
films my eye,
and every surface
of my skin
welcomes the mute, sad
ink stain in.

Each stark initial here
is mine:
carved crookedly
on cupboard door
and desk and chair . . .
scratched on the slim
long panels
of the echoing gym
and on the Art room's
painted floor.

I am the past
of boys who come
and go, but no one
calls my name:
each year, I have
a different one –
am in a different
image cast –
yet stay eternally
the same.

Jean Kenward

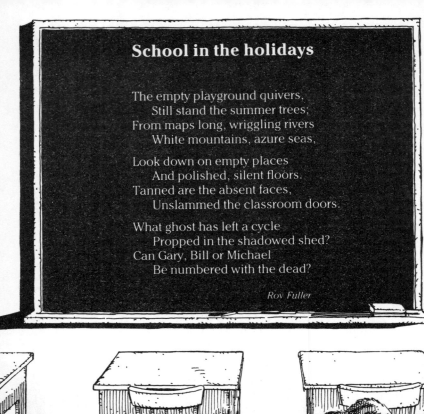

School in the holidays

The empty playground quivers,
    Still stand the summer trees;
From maps long, wriggling rivers
    White mountains, azure seas,

Look down on empty places
    And polished, silent floors.
Tanned are the absent faces,
    Unslammed the classroom doors.

What ghost has left a cycle
    Propped in the shadowed shed?
Can Gary, Bill or Michael
    Be numbered with the dead?

Roy Fuller

Holidays

Loading of our caravan,
Lifting, dragging, carting,
Holidays, dear holidays.
Starting,
      starting,
            starting.

Weather forecast; fine and cool.
Salty winds are blowing.
Not a word or thought of school.
We're going,
      going,
            GOING!

Carnivals along the coast,
Deck chairs, coloured brollies,
Marmalade and morning toast,
Fish and chips and lollies.

Where our bounding sea dog goes,
Where the netter dabs,
Pincering the tips of toes . . .
Irritated crabs.

Bring a bucket and a spade.
Hardly time to stop,
Bands upon the promenade,
Radios and Pop.

Trips around the tossing bay.
Climbing, leaping, chasing,
How the hours will fly away
Racing,
      racing,
            racing.

Back along the motorways,
Caravans are wending.
Holidays, dear holidays.
Ending,
      ending,
            ending.

Max Fatchen

Index of titles and first lines

first lines appear in *italic* print

Index of authors

Acknowledgements

The editor and publisher are grateful for permission to include the following copyright material in this anthology:

John Agard: 'Early Bird Does Catch the Fattest Worm', reprinted from *Say It again, Granny!* illustrated by Susanna Gretz, by permission of The Bodley Head. **Allan Ahlberg:** 'Blame' and 'Picking Teams' reprinted from *Please Mrs Butler* (Kestrel Books, 1983), copyright © 1983 by Allan Ahlberg, by permission of Penguin Books Ltd. **Dave Alton:** 'Learning' and 'Lesson in History', both © 1988 and reprinted by permission of the author. **Moira Andrew:** 'It's the thought that counts'. Reprinted by permission of the author. **Pam Ayres:** 'I don't want to go to school, mum' reprinted from *Thoughts of a Late Night Knitter*, copyright © Pam Ayres, by permission. **Valerie Bloom:** 'Tables'. Reprinted by permission of the author. **Alan Brownjohn:** 'The Rain Diary', reprinted by permission of the author. **Stanley Cook:** '47 Bus', 'School Dinner', 'The Reserve', 'The Exercise Book' and 'Squares', all © 1988 Stanley Cook and reprinted by permission of the author. **Nigel J Cox:** 'New Boy', © 1988 N J Cox, reprinted by permission of the author. **Philip C. Gross:** 'Scoo-wool-the hippiest time of your life', 'In Summer at break we play cricket' and 'The music examiner stood . . .', all © 1988 Philip C Gross and reprinted by permission of the author. **John Cunliffe:** 'You're standing on a strawberry' reprinted from *Standing on a Strawberry* by permission of André Deutsch Ltd. **Peter Dixon:** 'Wet Playtime', 'Teachers', 'The Colour of my Dreams', 'London Trip' and 'Where Do All the Teachers Go . . . ?, all © 1988 Peter Dixon. 'King of the Toilets' from *Nine O'Clock Bell*, ed. Raymond Wilson (Hutchinson). All reprinted by permission of the author. **Berlie Doherty:** 'Kieran' and 'I Hear . . . ', both © 1988 Berlie Doherty and reprinted with her permission. **David Durham:** 'Daydreamer', from *You'll Like This Stuff* edited by Morag Styles (Cambridge University Press 1986). Reprinted by permission of the author. **Max Fatchen:** 'Look Out' reprinted from *Songs for My Dog and Other People* (Kestrel Books, 1980), copyright © 1980 by Max Fatchen, by permission of Penguin Books Ltd, and John Johnson Ltd. 'News Break' and 'Holiday' are both © 1987 Max Fatchen and are reprinted by permission of John Johnson Ltd. **Eric Finney:** 'Monday' and 'Progress Report', both © 1988 Eric Finney and reprinted by permission of the author. **Frank Flynn:** 'Bad Habit', 'Never Say Boo to a Mouse' and 'A Flash of Moonlight on a Sunny Afternoon' are all © 1988 Frank Flynn and are reprinted with his permission. 'But I Didn't' is reprinted from *The Candy Floss Tree* by permission of the author and Oxford University Press. **Roy Fuller:** 'School in the Holidays', © 1988 Roy Fuller and reprinted with his permission. **Nigel Gray:** 'Summing Up', © 1988 Nigel Gray and reprinted with his permission. **David Harmer:** 'Some Days', 'Playtime in the Fog', 'It's not fair' and 'Exams', all © 1988 David Harmer and reprinted with his permission. **Gregory Harrison:** 'Lining Up', 'Morning Assembly', 'Swimming Lesson' and 'Playtime – Staying In', all © 1988 Gregory Harrison and reprinted with his permission. **Julie Holder:** 'Until the Bell', © 1988 Julie Holder and reprinted with her permission. **Geoffrey Holloway:** 'Swot', © 1988 Geoffrey Holloway and reprinted with his permission. **David Jackson:** 'Can You Keep a Secret?', 'Where's Your Homework?' and 'The Day of the Great Frost', all © 1988 David Jackson. **Jean Kenward:** 'Fear', 'The Outsider', 'The Miscreant', 'The Bite', 'Dissection', 'Going Home' and 'The Ghost' are all © 1988 Jean Kenward and are reprinted with her permission. **James Kirkup:** 'First Art Lesson', 'Extra-Curricular Activity', 'Poem To Be Buried In a Time Capsule', 'School Sports Day' and 'A Snowy Day at School' are all © 1988 James Kirkup and are reprinted with his permission. **John Kitching:** 'It's not my fault . . .', 'My teacher taught me how to see' and 'Computer Time', all © 1988 John Kitching and reprinted with his permission. **Ian McMillan and Martyn Wiley:** 'The hole in the hall', 'Trips' and 'My Long Scarf', © Ian McMillan and Martyn Wiley and reprinted with their permission. **Wes Magee:** 'Morning Break'. Reprinted by permission of the author. **Ray Mather:** 'Schoolspeak', 'Comparisons' and 'Homework' are all © 1988 Ray Mather and reprinted with his permission. **Trevor Millum:** 'Timetable' and 'The Song of the Homeworkers', both © Trevor Millum 1988 and reprinted with his permission. **Adrian Mitchell:** 'Two-Minute Girl' and 'The Blackboard' reprinted from *Nothingmas Day*, by permission of Allison & Busby Ltd., Publishers. **John Mole:** 'Mr Cartwright's Counting Rhyme' from *Our Ship*. Reprinted by permission of Secker & Warburg Ltd. **Judith Nicholls:** 'Late', 'School Dinners' ('The greater-spotted brown baked bean . . .') and 'Teacher Said' are from *Magic Mirror and Other Poems for Children* (Faber), © 1985 Judith Nicholls; 'Partners', '4 p.m.', 'Function Machine' and 'School Dinners' ('Sausages, Carrots . . .') all © 1988 Judith Nicholls. All poems reprinted by permission of the author. **Leslie Norris:** 'The Thin Prison' is reprinted from *Drumming in the Sky*, ed. Paddy Bechely (BBC Publications) by permission of the author. **Gareth Owen:** 'Drama Lesson' © 1986 Gareth Owen, first published in *Bright Lights Blaze Out*, poems by Alan Bold, Julie

O'Callaghan and Gareth Owen (OUP, 1986); 'Dear Mr Examiner' © 1988 Gareth Owen. Both reprinted with his permission. **Brian Patten:** 'The School Caretaker' and 'Zonky Zizzibug' reprinted from *Gargling with Jelly* (Viking Kestrel Books, 1985), copyright © Brian Patten 1985, by permission of Penguin Books Ltd., and the author. **John Rice:** 'A pencil case', 'My Teacher Said "Write a Poem About Fossils"' and 'Making the Grade', all © 1988 John Rice and reprinted with his permission. **Michael Rosen:** 'Unfair' reprinted from *Quick Let's Get Out of Here* by permission of André Deutsch Ltd. **Ian Serraillier:** 'Bus', 'Changing Gear' and 'School Dinner Rhyme' all © 1988 Ian Serraillier and reprinted with his permission. **Iain Crichton Smith:** 'August Poem', reprinted by permission of the author. **Derek Stuart:** 'Writing and Sums' and 'I am a full stop' are both © 1988 Derek Stuart and reprinted by permission of the author. **Odette Thomas:** 'Confusion' reprinted from *Rain Falling, Sun Shining* by permission of Bogle-L'Ouverture Publications Ltd. **Judith Thurman:** 'New Notebook' reprinted from *Flashlight and Other Poems,* copyright © 1976 by Judith Thurman, by permission of Penguin Books Ltd., and Atheneum Publishers, Inc. **J. J. Webster:** 'A Visit to the Zoo', © 1988 J. J. Webster and reprinted with his permission. **Colin West:** 'Ben', 'Plodders' and 'Winter Term', all © 1988 Colin West and reprinted with his permission. **Raymond Wilson:** 'Playground game', 'School Inspection' and 'Forget It!', all © 1988 Raymond Wilson and reprinted with his permission.

. . . and thanks to all school kids, past, present and future.